SURVIVAL SKILLS

Jenny Mason

Children's Press®
An imprint of Scholastic Inc.

SAFETY NOTE

This book suggests several survival skills techniques.
When possible, they should all be done with adult
supervision. Observe safety and caution at all times.
The author and publisher disclaim all liability for any
damage, mishap, injury, illness, or death that may
occur from engaging in the survival skills techniques
featured in this book or any other use of this book.

Special thanks to our content consultant, Ben McNutt, who has been teaching wilderness bushcraft and survival skills while leading remote expeditions to forest, jungle, desert, and frozen environments for more than 20 years. Ben also runs courses at wildhuman.com.

Library of Congress Cataloging-in-Publication Data
Names: Mason, Jenny (Children's author), author. | Francis, Kate, 1976– illustrator.
Title: Navigation / by Jenny Mason ; illustrations by Kate Francis.
Description: First edition. | New York, NY: Children's Press, an imprint of Scholastic Inc., 2023. | Series:
    A true book: Survival skills | Includes bibliographical references and index. | Audience: Ages 8–10. |
    Audience: Grades 4–6. | Summary: "A new installment in the A True Book series focusing on Survival
    Skills"— Provided by publisher.
Identifiers: LCCN 2022022735 (print) | LCCN 2022022736 (ebook) | ISBN 9781338853735 (library binding)
    | ISBN 9781338853742 (paperback) | ISBN 9781338853759 (ebk)
Subjects: LCSH: Navigation—Juvenile literature. | Maps—Symbols—Juvenile literature. | Compass—Juvenile
    literature. | Survival—Juvenile literature. | BISAC: JUVENILE NONFICTION / Sports & Recreation /
    Camping & Outdoor Activities | JUVENILE NONFICTION / General
Classification: LCC VK559.3 .M37 2023 (print) | LCC VK559.3 (ebook) | DDC 623.89—dc23/eng/20220708
LC record available at https://lccn.loc.gov/2022022735
LC ebook record available at https://lccn.loc.gov/2022022736

10 9 8 7 6 5 4 3 2 1   23 24 25 26 27

Printed in China, 62
First edition, 2023

Design by Kathleen Petelinsek
Series produced by Spooky Cheetah Press

Find the Truth!

Everything you are about to read is true *except* for one of the sentences on this page.

Which one is **TRUE**?

T or F South-facing mountain slopes usually have thicker vegetation than north-facing.

T or F A compass always points south.

Find the answers in this book.

What's in This Book?

Today, many people rely on GPS for navigating.

The **BIG** Truth

Lost in the Wilderness

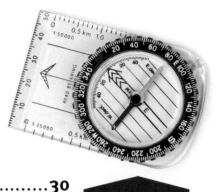

A compass can help us find our way.

4 High-Tech Tools & Advanced Skills

Stacks of rocks called cairns serve as guideposts on wilderness trails.

When the Wild Calls

Can you hear that? The great outdoors is calling, and it promises adventure! Before you run off, **be prepared**. Make sure to pack the essentials. That includes **water, snacks, sturdy walking shoes, and layered clothes** for when the sun sizzles or the rain drizzles. Last but not least, remember your trusty **navigation skills**!

Navigation is the science of moving safely and efficiently from one place to another. The best navigators can strike out, explore an unfamiliar area, and return home safely. With practice, you too can learn to be a **master navigator**.

Knowing how to navigate will give you the confidence to go exploring.

You can find cardinal directions on street signs, buildings, and wilderness maps.

Being able to navigate is a skill you will use throughout your life.

Cardinal Directions

North (N), south (S), east (E), and west (W). Those are the four cardinal, or main, directions anywhere in the world. Do you know which direction you're facing when you step out the front door? How about the direction you travel to school or a favorite park? Determining your location and the direction you take to the places you want to go is a key navigation skill. The first navigation tools people used were supplied by nature.

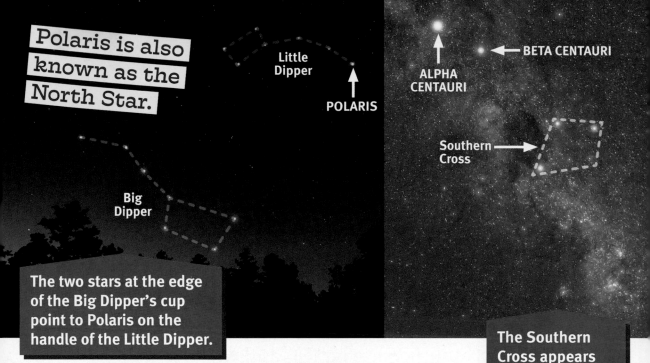

Little Dipper

POLARIS

ALPHA CENTAURI

← BETA CENTAURI

Southern Cross →

Big Dipper

The two stars at the edge of the Big Dipper's cup point to Polaris on the handle of the Little Dipper.

The Southern Cross appears like a bright kite.

Starlight, Star Bright

For centuries, people used the stars to find the cardinal directions. That is called celestial navigation. In the Northern **Hemisphere**, Polaris indicates due north, or exact north. This star remains in a mostly fixed location. The other stars in the night sky circle around it. In the Southern Hemisphere, navigators use the Southern Cross constellation and two bright pointer stars called Alpha and Beta Centauri to find due south.

Inherit the Stars

For tens of thousands of years, Indigenous Polynesian peoples used celestial navigation to explore islands flung across the Southern Pacific. From childhood, these clever sailors memorized all the constellations. They also studied cloud shapes and animal migrations to navigate. Later, their techniques helped European sailors venture across the world's vast oceans. Today, pilots and sailors still use these ancient methods as a backup to modern technology.

Polynesian sailors traveled in wakas, or voyaging canoes, like the modern reproduction shown here.

Sun Tracking

By day, the sun makes orienting easy. It rises along the eastern horizon. It sets roughly to the west. Daytime shadows can indicate cardinal directions. In the Northern Hemisphere, the sun tracks across the southern end of the sky. As a result, all shadows cast at midday point due north. Midday shadows in the Southern Hemisphere point due south. At the equator, the sun passes directly overhead. Therefore, shadows will nearly disappear by midday.

Can you tell where the sun is by looking at your shadow?

HOW TO PLOT DIRECTIONS USING SHADOWS

1. Poke a long stick into the dirt and tie a string or a shoelace to it.

2. Hold on to the string and move it in a circle around the stick. As you do, use your finger or a stick to trace a circle in the dirt.

3. At midday (between noon and 2:00 p.m.), place a pebble on the spot where the stick's shadow falls on the circle. If you are in the Northern Hemisphere, that shadow points north. Now you can plot out the other three cardinal directions.

A shadow is cast when a solid object blocks the light from a light source.

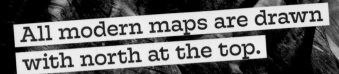
All modern maps are drawn with north at the top.

Navigators are cut off from the sun and stars inside slot canyons like this one. They need additional tools and skills.

Reading a Map

Maps are reliable navigation tools. You can use them to make quick decisions about where to go without waiting for the sun or stars to move. Maps are drawings or diagrams of particular places. They can represent cities, continents, or even the ocean floor. Today's navigation maps are printed on special paper blended with plastic. They are waterproof and do not rip. This way, they work anywhere, anytime.

Using Topographic Maps

Maps are flat, but Earth's surface is not. It swells and dips with mountains, valleys, and canyons. Topographic maps use contour lines to show these **terrain** shapes on a flat surface.

Reading a Topographic Map

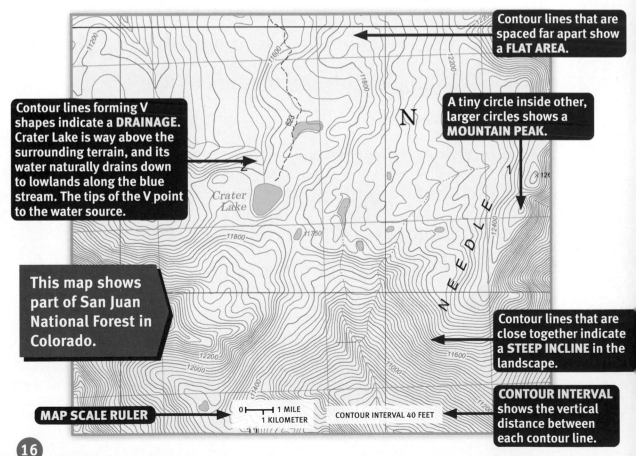

Contour lines that are spaced far apart show a **FLAT AREA**.

Contour lines forming V shapes indicate a **DRAINAGE**. Crater Lake is way above the surrounding terrain, and its water naturally drains down to lowlands along the blue stream. The tips of the V point to the water source.

A tiny circle inside other, larger circles shows a **MOUNTAIN PEAK**.

This map shows part of San Juan National Forest in Colorado.

Contour lines that are close together indicate a **STEEP INCLINE** in the landscape.

MAP SCALE RULER

0 ⊢——⊣ 1 MILE
1 KILOMETER

CONTOUR INTERVAL 40 FEET

CONTOUR INTERVAL shows the vertical distance between each contour line.

Scales and Distances

To fit real-world areas on a sheet of paper, mapmakers have to scale down the distances. Most topographic maps are on a 1:24,000 scale. That means 1 inch (2.5 centimeters) on a map represents 24,000 inches (61,000 cm)—or 1/4 mile (0.4 kilometer)—in the real world.

HOW TO MEASURE DISTANCE ON A MAP

1 Use a non-stretchy string to trace any trail on a map.

2 Using both hands, hold the string at the trail's start and finish points.

3 Without changing the position of your fingers, straighten the string segment over the map scale ruler and add up the miles.

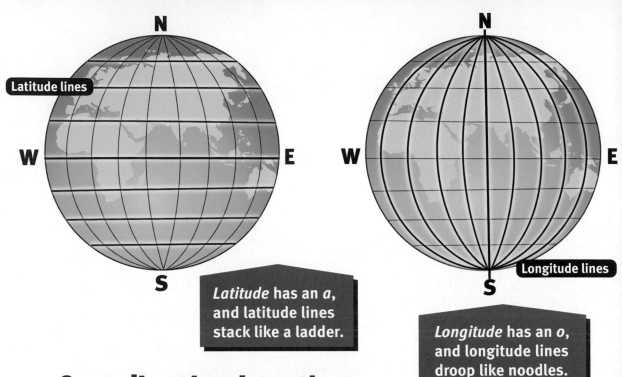

Latitude lines

Longitude lines

Latitude has an *a*, and latitude lines stack like a ladder.

Longitude has an *o*, and longitude lines droop like noodles.

Coordinating Locations

In addition to contour lines, topographic maps display grid lines. These imaginary lines wrap around the planet. Latitude lines circle the globe like belts. Longitude lines, or **meridians**, loop vertically from top to bottom. Your latitude changes as you move north or south. Your longitude changes as you travel east or west. You can pinpoint the location of anything on Earth using latitude and longitude **coordinates**.

Mercator's World

In 1569, mathematician Gerardus Mercator created the earliest and most accurate world map that used a projected mapping system. That means he projected Earth's round shape onto a flat surface. The Mercator world map remains the most familiar world map view.

The word *map* comes from *mappa*, the Latin word for "napkin" or "sheet."

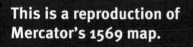
This is a reproduction of Mercator's 1569 map.

A Closer Look at Coordinates

Numbers are usually found all along a topographic map's outer edges. Those numbers identify latitude and longitude in degrees (°). Pick any location where the grid lines meet, and you know the coordinates of that place. Smaller measurements called minutes (') and seconds (") pinpoint locations between the grid lines. For example, the coordinates 63°4'10" N and 151°0'27" W precisely locate Denali, which is the highest mountain peak in North America.

In an emergency, rescue crews use coordinates to find you quickly.

Map of Alaska and surrounding areas

HOW TO NAVIGATE HIKING TRAILS WITH A MAP

1 When you arrive at the hiking trail, pinpoint your location on the map. The start of any trail is called a trailhead. Topographic maps show maintained trails and trailheads.

2 To find your coordinates, trace straight lines from your location to the map's edges.

3 To orient your map, lay the map on the ground or hold it horizontally. Identify landmarks around you. Landmarks include features such as lakes and mountains. Rotate the map until you can align the landmarks you see to those on the map.

4 As you walk along the trail, pause whenever the trail forks or intersects with other trails. Compare your **route** to your map so you do not take a wrong turn.

The compass we use today has changed very little since the 1400s.

A magnetic compass used for navigating was likely invented in Asia around the 11th century.

Using a Compass

Sometimes we can't see landmarks, or the terrain looks the same in all directions. That's when you should pair your map with a compass. A compass is a device that responds to Earth's **magnetic field**. Our planet has a solid iron core that is surrounded by molten (liquid) metal. Movement of the molten metal produces electric currents that create a magnetic field with invisible lines of force flowing north to south. A compass detects this magnetic field and helps people find the right direction to travel along.

Key Features of a Compass

Learning how to navigate with a compass begins with learning its main features.

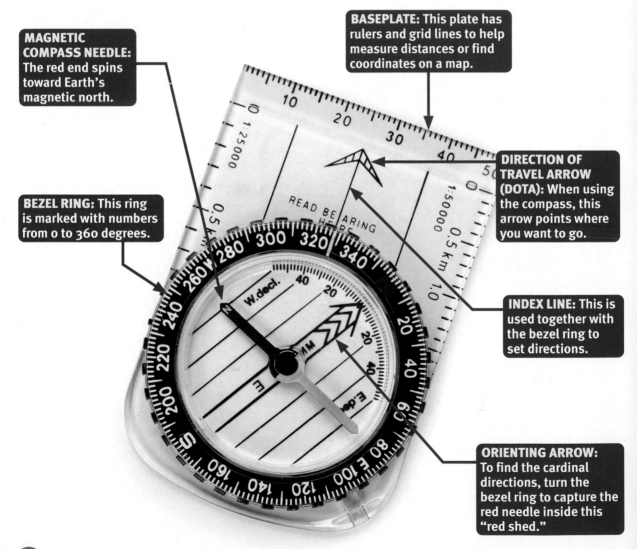

MAGNETIC COMPASS NEEDLE: The red end spins toward Earth's magnetic north.

BASEPLATE: This plate has rulers and grid lines to help measure distances or find coordinates on a map.

BEZEL RING: This ring is marked with numbers from 0 to 360 degrees.

DIRECTION OF TRAVEL ARROW (DOTA): When using the compass, this arrow points where you want to go.

INDEX LINE: This is used together with the bezel ring to set directions.

ORIENTING ARROW: To find the cardinal directions, turn the bezel ring to capture the red needle inside this "red shed."

True North Pole

Magnetic North Pole

N

S

The magnetic North Pole is several hundred miles from the true, or geographic, North Pole.

Magnetic North and True North

Before you use your compass, it needs a small adjustment. The needle points to the magnetic North Pole, which moves over time. You need to adjust your compass to find true north, which is the fixed, central top of the globe. The distance between true north and magnetic north is called **declination**. Current topographic maps show an area's declination. You can also look it up online. Different compass brands adjust for declination in different ways. Follow the directions for your compass.

Get Your Bearings

Taking a **bearing** is the first step when navigating with a map and compass. A bearing describes a precise direction using degrees.

HOW TO GET YOUR BEARINGS

1 Place the compass on your map. Trace a line from your location to your destination using the baseplate's longest edge. (Be sure the direction of travel arrow, or DOTA, points in the direction leading to the destination.)

2 Rotate the bezel ring until the N on the ring points to the N on the map. Remember: North is always at the top of the map.

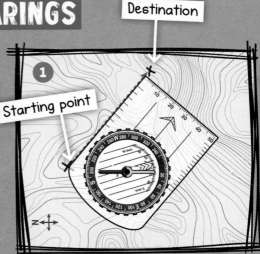

Destination

Starting point

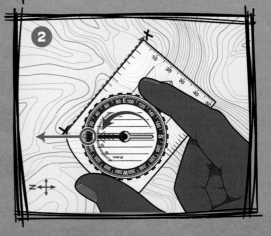

3 Note the bezel number at the index line. That is the bearing that will guide you to the destination.

4 Hold the compass flat on your hand with the DOTA facing away from you.

5 Rotate your whole body until the red end of the magnetic needle nests inside the orienting arrow. Navigators call this "boxing the needle" or "putting red in the shed."

6 Now you and your compass are facing your destination. You can travel without a trail so long as you follow your bearing. Pick a tree or another reachable landmark along the bearing. Travel to it. Repeat this process until you reach your destination.

Triangulate Your Location

In many wilderness areas, trails are built to safely guide people. Even so, hikers can easily lose track of trails while exploring or taking pictures. Snow or fallen trees can hide trails from view. Whenever you lose track of your trail, use your map and compass to pin down your location.

HOW TO TRIANGULATE YOUR LOCATION

1 Find three major landmarks spread out around you. Make sure each one appears on your map.

2 With your compass flat on your hand, point the DOTA at one landmark.

3 Turn the bezel ring to put "red in the shed." The bezel number at the index line is the bearing to that landmark.

Landmark 2

Landmark

1 3

Landmark 1

4 Place your map on the ground, set the compass on top, and point the DOTA at the landmark.

5 Move the baseplate until the N on the bezel ring points to the top of the map. Be sure the long edge of the compass still touches the landmark.

6 Draw a line on the map along the baseplate's edge to the landmark. You may need to move your compass along that line so you can use the edge to continue drawing a longer straight line.

7 Repeat steps 2 through 6 for the other two landmarks. The lines will form a triangle where they meet. Your location is at the center of the triangle.

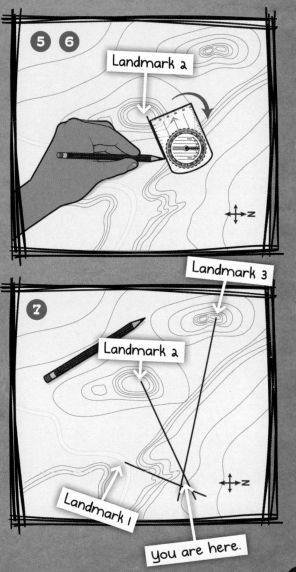

5 6

Landmark 2

N

7

Landmark 3

Landmark 2

Landmark 1

N

You are here.

Lost in the Wilderness

Even the most skilled navigators can get lost. They may have to veer off course because of sudden bad weather or damaged trails. They may lose track of time and go astray trying to navigate at night. If you are lost, the first thing you must do is stop moving. Then ask yourself these three questions. The answers will tell you what is best to do next.

1

Do you have a high level of navigation skills? That means you can skillfully navigate with orientation skills, bearings, and triangulation.

If yes: Answer the next question.

SIGNALS: Build a fire. Use mirrors or other reflectors (such as a cell phone screen, Mylar blanket, or aluminum foil) to flash sunlight, which can be seen for many miles. You can also blow a whistle or shout three times, then wait and listen. Repeat.

2

Do you have a high level of energy?
Energy refers to your physical condition based on how far you have traveled already, as well as any injuries. Energy also refers to your food and water supplies.

3

Is there a lot of daylight left?
Light is crucial for safely navigating. Avoid navigating at night, when you risk injuries from tripping or falling. Night is also the time when most predators roam.

If yes: Answer the next question.

If yes: Navigate back to safety.

If no: Stay put. Signal for help and gather needed supplies.

SUPPLIES: Essential supplies include shelter, fire, and water. How to build shelter and start a fire are survival skills that need to be learned. You should receive training for both. Always carry plenty of water when you are out exploring. If you need to find water in the wild, search lowlands where water pools. Look for moss or lush grasses. These plants may point to a spring. Any water collected in wild spaces must be sanitized. Boil it for 3 minutes before drinking. You can also melt snow to drink.

Modern location devices such as wristwatches and smartphones are tiny and light. Early devices were the size of a six-pack of drink cans.

Electronic devices are not 100 percent reliable.

CHAPTER 4

High-Tech Tools & Advanced Skills

Electronic gadgets that display digital maps have made navigation easier. At the push of a button, they triangulate your precise coordinates. They guide you through the wilderness. Yet even though they seem like magic, electronic devices have limitations. Sometimes their signals are blocked. Also, their batteries can run out of power. That is why a map and compass should serve as backup tools to these gadgets.

GPS technology was originally designed for use by the military. It became available to the public in 1983.

GPS satellites are visible at night as bright dots sailing across the sky. Unlike stars, they do not twinkle.

Global Positioning System (GPS)

The most common and easy-to-use modern navigation tool is the Global Positioning System (GPS). This system is a network of 31 **satellites** swirling around the planet. Each satellite circles Earth twice a day and sends data to receivers anywhere on the planet. GPS receivers are found in cars, smartphones, fitness trackers, and handheld navigation units.

Navigating with GPS

Handheld GPS units can be used for navigating in the wild. There are many different handheld units you can buy. Be sure to read the instruction manual for your unit. In general, a GPS unit acts as a compass and map combined. A GPS unit can determine your location. To do this, the unit triangulates your location with data from four different satellites. Most units can display your position on a digital map. You can also view the longitude and latitude coordinates of your location.

Space weather, such as energy flares from the sun, can disrupt the radio waves beamed from GPS satellites.

Make sure to refresh your device as you move along a route.

Waypoints and Routes

Before starting any journey, be sure to find your route on your GPS unit. A route is a path you follow along many points, including starting points, midpoints, and end points. These different **waypoints** mark your way in the wild. When you arrive at a trailhead, turn on your GPS unit. With an adult's help, open the digital map on the GPS unit. Find the destination you want to reach. Tap or click this location to set a waypoint. Next, click "go" or "go to." The GPS unit then finds a route to the destination. Some units may display a trail. Compare the GPS route to your map's marked trails.

Some GPS units sound an alert if you veer off track.

Trailblazers

In many wild areas, local governments or outdoor volunteer clubs build trails that guide people into the wilderness. Trekkers must learn the trail markers that keep them on target. For instance, blazes are slash marks cut into tree trunks. Some blazes are painted on trees. Rock cairns, or stacked rocks, also guide people wherever a dirt trail cannot be seen. Always use these markers, plus your map and compass, to verify your GPS route.

Short cairns are also known as ducks.

A blaze might be painted on a tree.

Wild Secrets

The more you befriend the wilderness, the more it will share secrets that can help you navigate. One thing you can do is learn the wind patterns, or prevailing winds, in an area. Over time, these air currents bend trees in a particular direction. For example, if a steady wind blows south, trees will tilt southward. Noticing where plants grow can also help you navigate. South-facing slopes tend to have denser vegetation.

Timeline: Navigation Tools Throughout History

16,500 BCE
Cave paintings of a star map in France show that people were using the stars for navigation thousands of years ago.

3RD CENTURY BCE
The alidade is invented. It is a tool used to calculate distances on land.

2ND CENTURY CE
Astrolabes are invented. They can map the stars and tell time. Navigators still use astrolabes today.

1088
The magnetic compass is described for the first time, in China. In all likelihood, it was in use long before this mention.

38

The Way Forward

Knowing how to navigate in the wilderness is an essential skill. You can enjoy your time outdoors when you are not worried about getting lost. These skills can help you find your way around your neighborhood and city too. Be sure to practice using the tools and the methods before you set off. The time to master navigation is not when you are lost, cold, or running from predators. And remember: The more skills you know, the better your adventures can be.

6TH CENTURY
The theodolite is invented. It measures vertical and horizontal angles to find latitude and longitude. Theodolites are still used for mapping.

1757
The sextant is invented. It calculates longitude and latitude to pinpoint locations. Ships still carry sextants as a backup to GPS.

1978
The first GPS satellites are launched into outer space.

1983
GPS is made available to the public.

HIKER SURVIVES
Getting Lost in Snowstorm

Although he was tired and hungry, 73-year-old Gab Song survived.

On February 15, 2022, Gab Song set off to hike Mount Pinos in California's Los Padres National Forest.

Even though Song was familiar with the area, he packed a compass and map. He also layered his clothes and brought along extra food and water. Song told his family he planned to hike for a few hours. However, an unexpected snowstorm slammed the mountain. Cold, powdery drifts erased the trails. Song was soon lost.

As nighttime swallowed the forest, Song used all his survival skills to stay alive. He found shelter and built a fire. He melted snow to drink. In the morning, Song used his compass and map to triangulate his location. He noticed a nearby motorway on the map. Song determined a bearing to lead him to that road. Once there, he flagged down a passing car. After making some calls, Song learned that when he did not return as planned, his family alerted search and rescue teams (SAR). The teams connected with Song and took him home.

Song looks ready to head back out for future adventures!

Take this quiz to find out if you are ready to navigate the wilderness!

 1 Name the four cardinal directions.

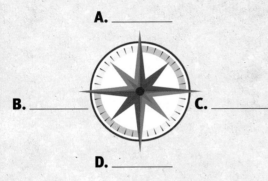

A. _____

B. _____

C. _____

D. _____

 2 In the Northern Hemisphere, in which direction do midday shadows point?

A. Southwest

B. North

C. Nowhere; they disappear

D. None of the above

 3 Lines of _____ track north and south navigation.

....

 4 Lines of _____ track east and west navigation.

....

 5 Which star indicates due north in the Northern Hemisphere?

A. Sirius

B. Polaris

C. Alpha Centauri

D. None of the above

Study this snippet from a topographic map to answer questions 6 through 8.

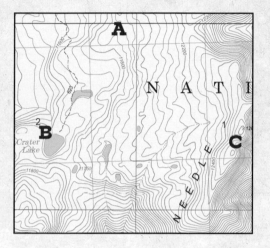

Study this map section to answer questions 9 and 10.

6 Does location A represent a steep incline or a flat area?

....

7 What is shown at point B?

....

8 What kind of feature is represented at point C?

9 Which town is closest to the coordinates of 70° N and 160° W?

....

10 What is the straight-line distance (in miles) between Nome and Fairbanks?

True Statistics

The percentage of all U.S. wilderness spaces available for public use: 32% (or 727 million acres)

The number of people exploring wilderness spaces in national parks and U.S. Forest Service (USFS) areas every year: 471 million

The size and weight of the world's largest atlas (a collection of printed maps): 6 feet (2 m) tall by 4.5 feet (1.4 m) wide; 440 pounds (200 kg)

The number of people around the world who adopted GPS for daily use by 2012: 526 million

The altitude at which GPS satellites orbit above Earth's surface: 12,550 miles (20,200 km)

Did you find the truth?

T South-facing mountain slopes usually have thicker vegetation than north-facing.

F A compass always points south.

Resources

Other books in this series:

You can also look at:

Cunningham, Kevin. *Reading Maps*. New York: Scholastic, 2012.

Cunningham, Kevin. *Types of Maps*. New York: Scholastic, 2012.

Graham, Ian. *You Wouldn't Want to Live Without Satellites!* New York: Scholastic, 2019.

Grylls, Bear. *Survival Skills Handbook*. Vol 1. Tulsa, OK: Kane Miller, 2017.

Glossary

bearing (BAIR-ing) the position of one point with respect to another, or its direction from another

coordinates (koh-OR-duh-nits) sets of numbers used to show the position of a point on a line, graph, or map

declination (deh-kluh-NAY-shuhn) the angular distance between magnetic north and true, or geographic, north

hemisphere (HEM-i-sfeer) one half of a round object, especially of the earth

magnetic field (mag-NET-ik feeld) the area around an electric current that has the power to attract other metals, usually iron or steel

meridians (muh-RID-ee-uhnz) imaginary circles on the earth's surface that pass through the North and South Poles and are used to show locations of places on Earth

route (ROOT or ROUT) a road, path, or course that you follow to get from one place to another

satellites (SAT-uh-lites) spacecraft that are sent into orbit around the earth, the moon, or another cosmic body

terrain (tuh-RAYN) an area of land

waypoints (WAY-points) two or more points on a route or line of travel

Index

Page numbers in **bold** indicate illustrations.

About the Author

Jenny Mason is a story-hunter. She explores foreign countries, canyon mazes, and burial crypts to gather the facts that make the best true tales. Her research knows no bounds. She once sniffed a 200-year-old rotten skull. Jenny received an MFA in Writing for Children and Young Adults from the Vermont College of Fine Arts. She also holds an MPhil from Trinity College Dublin. Find all her books and projects at jynnemason.com.